# ECOFACTS

# POLLUTION

## ECO FACTS

IZZI HOWELL

CRABTREE
PUBLISHING COMPANY
WWW.CRABTREEBOOKS.COM

# CRABTREE
## PUBLISHING COMPANY
### WWW.CRABTREEBOOKS.COM

**Author:** Izzi Howell

**Editorial director:** Kathy Middleton

**Editors:** Izzi Howell, Petrice Custance

**Proofreader:** Melissa Boyce

**Designer:** Clare Nicholas

**Cover designer:** Steve Mead

**Prepress technician:** Tammy McGarr

**Print coordinator:** Katherine Berti

**Photo credits:**
Getty: Aaron P. Bernstein 9b, Aryfahmed 11t, Jonathan Alcorn/ Bloomberg 13t, niewielki 14, Marccophoto 19, The Asahi Shimbun 25, JasonDoiy 29; NASA: Jacques Descloitres, MODIS Rapid Response Team, NASA/GSFC 21b; Shutterstock: nevenm 7, outdoorimages 9t, Robby Fakhriannur 17, sladkozaponi 21t, PRESSLAB 23; The Ocean Cleanup: Erwin Zwart/The Ocean Cleanup 11b, 13b.

All design elements from Shutterstock.

Every attempt has been made to clear copyright. Should there be any inadvertent omission please apply to the publisher for rectification.

The website addresses (URLs) included in this book were valid at the time of going to press. However, it is possible that contents or addresses may have changed since the publication of this book. No responsibility for any such changes can be accepted by either the author or the Publisher.

**Library and Archives Canada Cataloguing in Publication**

Title: Pollution eco facts / Izzi Howell.
Names: Howell, Izzi, author.
Description: Series statement: Eco facts | Includes index.
Identifiers: Canadiana (print) 20190087897 |
  Canadiana (ebook) 20190087900 |
  ISBN 9780778763550 (hardcover) |
  ISBN 9780778763659 (softcover) |
  ISBN 9781427123473 (HTML)
Subjects: LCSH: Pollution—Juvenile literature. | LCSH: Refuse and
  refuse disposal—Environmental aspects—Juvenile literature. |
  LCSH: Nature—Effect of human beings on—Juvenile literature.
Classification: LCC TD176 .H69 2019 | DDC j363.7—dc23

**Library of Congress Cataloging-in-Publication Data**

Names: Howell, Izzi, author.
Title: Pollution eco facts / Izzi Howell.
Description: New York : Crabtree Publishing Company, 2019. |
Series: Eco facts | Includes index. |
  Audience: Age 10-14+ | Audience: Grade 7 to 8. |
  Identifiers: LCCN 2019014216 (print) | LCCN 2019021712 (ebook) |
  ISBN 9781427123473 (Electronic) |
  ISBN 9780778763550 (hardcover) |
  ISBN 9780778763659 (pbk.)
Subjects: LCSH: Pollution--Juvenile literature.
Classification: LCC TD176 (ebook) | LCC TD176 .H68 2019 (print) |
  DDC 363.73--dc23
LC record available at https://lccn.loc.gov/2019014216

## Crabtree Publishing Company

www.crabtreebooks.com    1–800–387–7650

Published by Crabtree Publishing Company in 2020
©2019 The Watts Publishing Group.

Printed in the U.S.A./072019/CG20190501

**Published in Canada**
**Crabtree Publishing**
616 Welland Ave.
St. Catharines, Ontario
L2M 5V6

**Published in the United States**
**Crabtree Publishing**
PMB 59051
350 Fifth Avenue, 59th Floor
New York, New York 10118

# Contents

# What is pollution?

Pollution is damage done to the **environment** through the creation of waste and harmful or **toxic** substances. Most pollution is the result of human activity.

## Types

There are many types of pollution. Different activities affect the air, water, and land. Some activities also damage the environment by producing too much sound or light (see pages 26–27).

**sound pollution**

**water pollution**

Polluted air, soil, and water lead to the deaths of **9 million** people every year.

## Dangers

Pollution damages the natural world. It destroys **ecosystems** and harms the animals and plants that live in them. Pollution also affects people's health. Some types of pollution can hurt or even kill people, by leading to conditions such as lung disease and cancer.

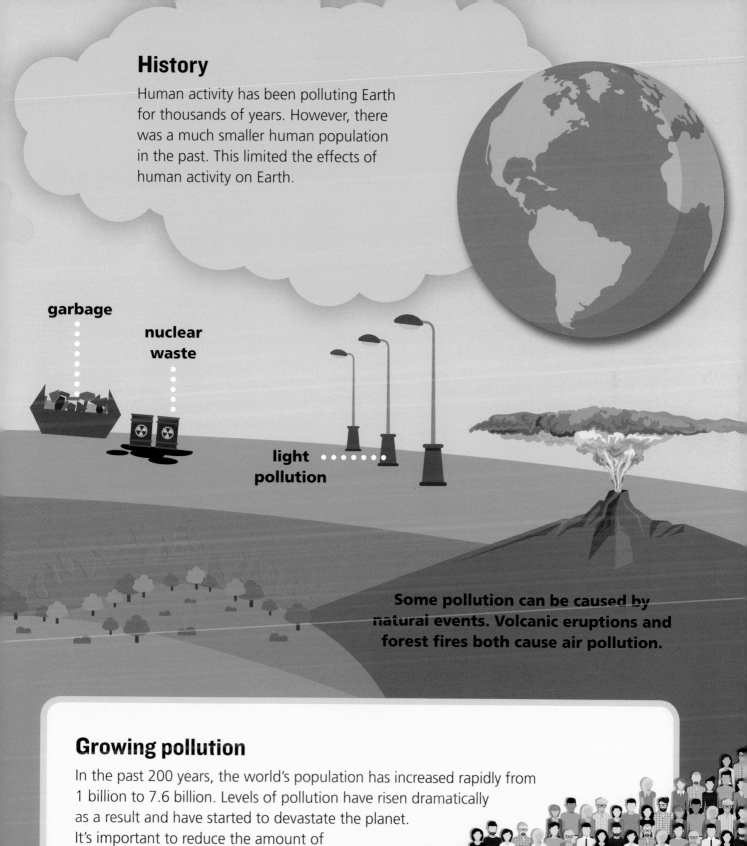

# History

Human activity has been polluting Earth for thousands of years. However, there was a much smaller human population in the past. This limited the effects of human activity on Earth.

**garbage**

**nuclear waste**

**light pollution**

Some pollution can be caused by natural events. Volcanic eruptions and forest fires both cause air pollution.

# Growing pollution

In the past 200 years, the world's population has increased rapidly from 1 billion to 7.6 billion. Levels of pollution have risen dramatically as a result and have started to devastate the planet. It's important to reduce the amount of pollution now to help **preserve** the natural world and protect our health.

# Water

Water can be polluted by **industry, fertilizers** from farming, and plastic and human waste. Water pollution affects our water supply, which we use for cooking and cleaning, and damages the **habitats** of aquatic plants and animals.

## Sources

In some areas, chemicals and waste are dumped directly into rivers and lakes through pipes. Sometimes, there are no rules to stop companies from polluting the water, or companies break the rules. In farming areas, fertilizers can soak through the soil and travel into bodies of water, or are washed into the water by rain.

## Living things

Animals and plants can be harmed, or even killed, by pollution in the water. When larger ocean animals, such as swordfish, eat small ocean animals that have **consumed** toxic substances, such as mercury, the poison passes into their bodies. As large animals eat so many smaller animals, they consume a large amount of poison. It can be dangerous for humans to eat too much of these fish, as the poison will affect them too.

**Amount of mercury**

| **200** krill | eaten by | **20** squid | eaten by | **10** mackerel | eaten by | **1** swordfish |

*These women in India are washing themselves and their clothes in the Ganges River. The Ganges River is one of the most polluted rivers in the world.*

## Human use

Many people in less economically developed countries are forced to use polluted water every day for washing, cooking, and drinking. This water often contains bacteria that can cause disease. Every year, 1.8 million people die as a result of drinking polluted water. Polluted water can also contain dangerous substances that humans should not consume, such as lead.

**70%** of industrial waste is dumped into water in developing countries.

## Water-poor countries

Less economically developed countries have the greatest demand for clean, fresh water. **Rural** areas often do not have piped clean water, and many places suffer from drought. These countries also have the fewest controls on industry and agriculture, so many companies dispose of their waste in water. Governments can't afford to **invest** in cleaning up pollution in rivers and lakes, which are the only sources of fresh water for some people.

## Solutions

To tackle the issue of water pollution, governments must create rules that stop industry and agriculture from letting chemicals and fertilizers run into lakes, rivers, and oceans. They should also pass laws to protect fresh water and oceans. This will allow governments to sue people who break the law and make them pay to clean it up.

# Lake Erie

Lake Erie is one of the five Great Lakes—a group of large lakes in the United States and Canada. Major cities, such as Cleveland, Ohio, and Buffalo, New York, as well as many factories, are built on its banks. This led to a serious pollution problem in the 1960s.

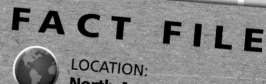

**FACT FILE**

LOCATION:
**North America**

SIZE:
**9,910 square miles (25,667 sq km)**

AVERAGE DEPTH:
**62 feet (19 m)**

**Lake Erie**

## Sources of pollution

The area around Lake Erie is very industrial. In the past, oil and waste from industry were dumped into the lake and its **tributaries**, as there were no rules about water pollution. The lake's tributaries also pass through huge areas of farmland. Fertilizers used on the farms got into the water through the soil or were washed into the water when it rained.

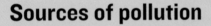

*Fertilizers from farming have caused problems in Lake Erie. Just as fertilizers make crops grow faster, they also make a type of toxic **algae** grow very quickly.*

**1** *The toxic algae covers the surface of the water, blocking light from reaching underwater plants.*

**2** *The underwater plants die, as they cannot carry out **photosynthesis** without light.*

**3** *This destroys the lake's ecosystem, as **herbivores**, such as small fish, do not have any plants to eat.*

## Dead zones

A dead zone is an area of water with very little oxygen. Nothing can live there. Toxic algae has created many dead zones in Lake Erie. When plants die underwater, their remains **decompose**, which uses up oxygen in the water. So many plants died because of toxic algae in Lake Erie that nearly all the oxygen in the water was removed. Oxygen levels in the water dropped so low that fish suffocated and died.

## Cuyahoga success story

The Cuyahoga River is a tributary of Lake Erie. It was once one of the most polluted rivers in the United States, filled with trash and oil from the factories that lined its banks. Over the past 30 years, the water quality has improved, thanks to new laws controlling the release of waste into water.

*The areas around some sections of the Cuyahoga River were protected in the 1970s. Nothing can be built on the riverbanks there.*

## Saving Lake Erie

The pollution in Lake Erie inspired the creation of two new laws in the 1970s. These laws forced the government to provide funding to clean up the lake and to put pressure on factories to stop polluting it. Today, the lake is much cleaner and is popular with tourists and fishers. However, toxic algae continues to affect some parts of the lake. Even just a small amount of fertilizer from farms has a huge impact on the lake's health.

**The Cuyahoga River contained so much oil that it caught fire on at least 13 different occasions!**

*In 2014, algae became a serious problem again in Lake Erie. People in the area were banned from drinking tap water (which comes from the lake) for two days because there was so much algae in it.*

# Ocean plastic

Every year, around 14 million tons (12.7 million metric tons) of plastic pollution ends up in the ocean. This plastic damages the ocean habitat and kills and injures animals that live there.

Every minute, the equivalent of a garbage truck full of plastic is dumped into the ocean.

## Journey to the sea

The wind can blow lightweight plastic from landfills into the water. Plastic products, such as cotton swabs, are flushed down toilets and end up in the ocean. Some companies throw plastic waste straight into the ocean.

*Some drainpipes carry plastic into the ocean.*

### One small step

When you visit the beach, try to pick up at least 10 pieces of plastic litter. This will stop the trash from being pulled back into the ocean by the **tide**. Recycle as much of the litter as possible.

## Spreading far and wide

Once plastic is in the ocean, it is carried along by waves and currents. Plastic ends up in every part of the ocean, from deep-sea trenches to polar ice caps. It will remain in the ocean for many years, as plastic does not break down easily.

## Big and small

Animals get trapped in large pieces of plastic, which can result in drowning. Some ocean animals eat floating plastic bags as they mistake them for sea jellies. The plastic bags damage their stomach. Animals also eat small, sharp pieces of plastic that can cut open their stomach.

*This sea turtle is tangled in plastic netting.*

**There are approximately**
**5,000,000,000,000**
**(5 trillion) pieces of plastic in the ocean.**

## Banning microbeads

Some countries have recently banned plastic microbeads. These are tiny balls of plastic added to products used for scrubbing the skin. These plastic balls can end up in the ocean, where they are eaten by animals.

## Removing plastic

Reducing the amount of plastic waste that we produce means that less plastic will end up in the ocean. However, it's also important to remove the plastic that is already there. The Ocean Cleanup project has created a solar-powered floating barrier that will move through the ocean, pushing floating plastic pieces to shore.

## Recycling ocean plastic

Some companies have started to find ways to recycle ocean plastic. One clothing manufacturer has brought out a range of shoes with soles made from recycled ocean plastic. Another company is using ocean plastic to make frames for glasses.

# FOCUS ON
# The Great Pacific Garbage Patch

The Great Pacific Garbage Patch is a huge area of plastic pollution in the Pacific Ocean. Most of the pieces of plastic are tiny microplastics.

## FACT FILE

 **LOCATION:**
Pacific Ocean

 **SIZE:**
618,000 square miles
(1.6 million sq km)

 **THREAT TO:**
All ocean animals, including seabirds and mammals

Japan

gyre

Hawaii

California

*The Great Pacific Garbage Patch can be divided into two parts: the Western Garbage Patch, near Japan, and the Eastern Garbage Patch, between California and Hawaii.*

## Gyres

The Great Pacific Garbage Patch is inside an ocean gyre. A gyre is a circular system of ocean **currents**. The water moves clockwise around the gyre. This movement pulls garbage from the Pacific Ocean into the center of the gyre.

## Spotting plastic

Sailors traveling through the Great Pacific Garbage Patch may not notice much plastic, as the pieces of microplastic are too small to be seen by the naked eye. Water containing microplastic just looks cloudy. However, there are many large pieces of plastic in some areas. Plastic can also sink to the ocean floor.

## Origins

Eighty percent of the plastic in the Great Pacific Garbage Patch comes from North America and Asia. The rest comes from boats that dump garbage straight into the ocean or lose their **cargo** accidentally.

Marine researcher Charles Moore holds a tray of plastic that has washed ashore in Hawaii. Moore was the first person to identify the patch in 1997.

## Threats

Many animals die as a result of eating plastic (see page 11). Large ocean mammals get trapped in abandoned fishing nets and drown, as they need to visit the ocean's surface to breathe.

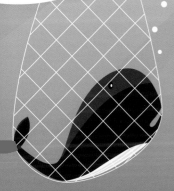

## Ocean food chains

Plastic blocks sunlight from reaching algae and **plankton**, which stops them from carrying out photosynthesis and growing. Less algae and plankton means less food for plant-eating animals at the bottom of the food chain. If these animals die, **carnivores** at the top of the food chain will also go hungry.

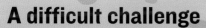

## A difficult challenge

As the Great Pacific Garbage Patch is far from the coastline of any country, many governments do not see it as their problem. It is also difficult to clean up the area as the plastic constantly moves with the waves and is spread across a huge area.

## Cleaning up

There are several charities and organizations that are trying to clean up the patch. The Ocean Cleanup project has used ships with very fine nets to trap and remove tiny bits of microplastic.

An Ocean Cleanup ship collects nets from the Great Pacific Garbage Patch.

# Waste Disposal

Waste that can't be reused or recycled, such as some plastics and electronic waste, is sent to dumps or landfill sites. The waste in these sites does not break down quickly, and remains in the ground for many years.

## Dumps

A dump is an open hole in the ground where garbage is placed. It is usually a smelly, dirty place where diseases can spread. Dumps are more common in less economically developed countries that can't afford more efficient waste-disposal systems. Some more economically developed countries pay less economically developed countries to take their waste and dispose of it in dumps.

*In an electronic waste site in Ghana, people look for valuable metal waste to sell. They burn the waste to expose copper wires and pieces. This creates toxic air pollution.*

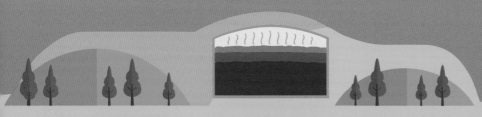

## Landfill

A landfill is a structure built into the ground where garbage is placed. It is lined so that the garbage is not in contact with the soil. When the landfill is full, it is covered with soil so that it can't be seen.

## Problems

Even though landfill sites aren't visible, the land they cover can't be used for any other purpose. This reduces the area available for homes and other buildings. If the lining of the landfill breaks, chemicals from the garbage can leak into the ground. This pollution can travel to the surface and poison plants and animals.

## Long-term waste

Most objects that we put into landfill sites, such as plastic, will take hundreds or even thousands of years to decompose. Throwing these objects away is not a long-term solution, as we will run out of landfill space long before these objects break down.

## Dangerous gases

When some garbage decomposes, it produces methane, which is a **greenhouse gas** (see page 18). Methane is very flammable, which increases the risk of explosions at dumps. In some places, people burn garbage rather than place it in dumps or landfills. This creates dangerous gases and air pollution, which leads to health problems for people living nearby.

**By 2050, 13 billion tons (11.8 billion metric tons) of plastic will be placed in landfills.**

## Compost and recycling

Some types of waste can be **composted** or recycled rather than being sent to landfill sites. Food waste can be left to decompose and then turned into compost. This compost can be used as fertilizer to help plants grow well.

*Paper, glass, metal, and many types of plastic can be recycled.*

## One small step

**Find out what items can be recycled in your area. Try to recycle as much as possible, even small things, such as batteries.**

15

# Air

Air pollution is made up of gases and tiny particles that are released into the air. They can affect the health of living things that breathe them in.

**9 out of 10** people around the world breathe polluted air.

## Sources of pollution

Air pollution comes from different sources, such as power plants that burn **fossil fuels** for energy. Air pollution is also created by vehicles that run on gasoline and diesel fuels, such as planes, cars, and trucks. These sources create polluting smoke and fumes that release toxic gases and tiny particles into the air.

## Natural air pollution

Some natural events can pollute the air that we breathe. Strong winds pick up dust and sand, which can be irritating if breathed in. Wildfires and volcanic eruptions produce huge clouds of smoke that can cause breathing problems.

# Indoor air pollution

Around 3 billion people burn **biomass** or coal inside their homes for cooking and heating. Burning these fuels creates indoor pollution. Many of these people live in less economically developed countries, where they don't have reliable access to electricity.

*Indoor air pollution is particularly damaging to people's health, as the pollution gets trapped inside the home and breathed in continuously.*

## Health risks

When people breathe in polluted air, tiny particles travel into the lungs and bloodstream. Long-term exposure to air pollution can cause breathing problems and allergies. It can make conditions such as asthma worse, and even lead to serious illnesses such as lung disease and cancer.

## Problem areas

Many less economically developed countries have serious problems with air pollution. The governments in these countries rely on polluting industries to make money. Although these factories are damaging people's health, some governments can't afford to limit industries and force them to pollute less. As they see it, the only way to eventually afford clean but expensive new technology is to continue earning money through polluting industries.

## Breathing clean

There are various ways to help reduce air pollution. Clean sources of energy, such as solar, wind, and **tidal power**, can be used to create electricity. Congestion charges can be used in cities to reduce the number of vehicles on the road. Using electric vehicles, which create no fumes, would help to reduce air pollution further.

## One small step

**Walk or cycle instead of driving. For longer trips, use public transportation.**

# The greenhouse effect

The greenhouse effect is one of the most damaging consequences of air pollution. It results in an increase in Earth's temperature, which leads to **climate change**.

## Greenhouse gases

The greenhouse effect is caused by certain gases, known as greenhouse gases. They include carbon dioxide ($CO_2$), methane, and nitrous oxide. Greenhouse gases are released naturally on Earth. However, these gases are also being released at dangerously high levels through human activity.

CO₂

## The atmosphere

After they are released, greenhouse gases gather in the **atmosphere** above the surface of Earth. They trap heat energy from the Sun close to the surface of Earth.

*Most of the heat from the Sun is trapped by the atmosphere. Only a small amount can escape back into space.*

## Natural greenhouse gases

The greenhouse effect is natural. Greenhouse gases are released when humans and animals breathe out carbon dioxide. They are also released when volcanoes erupt and spew out carbon dioxide and water vapor. Having these gases in the atmosphere keeps Earth warm enough for life to exist.

## Hotter and hotter

Human activity, such as the burning of fossil fuels, is producing far more greenhouse gases than naturally exist on Earth. As a result, more heat is being trapped near Earth's surface. This is causing the planet's temperature to increase beyond a healthy temperature. Since 1880, it has risen 1.62 °F (0.9 °C). This may not sound like a lot, but it is enough to cause major worldwide damage.

## Climate change

The rising temperature on Earth is affecting the natural environment. Ice is melting at the poles, destroying polar habitats and making sea levels rise around the world. The high temperatures are leading to more extreme weather conditions, such as hurricanes. They are also changing rainfall patterns and increasing drought in many areas.

Since 1880, global sea levels have risen **9 inches (23 cm).**

## Impact

If greenhouse gases continue to be released at current rates, climate change on Earth will become more severe. This will have a serious impact on all life on Earth. Many coastal areas will be flooded and people will have to leave their homes. Our food supply will be affected by drought or very heavy rains. It's important for us to reduce air pollution to control the greenhouse effect, as well as to improve our health.

*This field of corn has been destroyed by drought.*

# FOCUS ON

# Air pollution in India

India contains some of the most polluted areas in the world. Cities are polluted by factories, homes, and vehicles packed in close together. Rural areas are affected by indoor air pollution and crop burning.

## Rural areas

Two-thirds of India's population live in rural areas. The majority of these people, around 80 percent, burn biomass for cooking and heating. This adds up to a huge amount of air pollution. When crops have been **harvested**, farmers often burn the plants to clear them away, which creates additional air pollution.

## Cities

Cities in India produce their own pollution, as well as being affected by pollution that drifts in from the countryside. Dust from new construction projects and fumes from factories and vehicles combine to create highly polluted conditions.

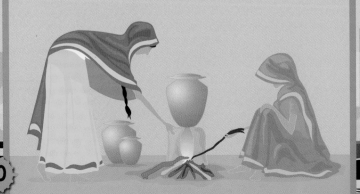

*Traffic jams create additional air pollution if drivers do not turn off their engines while waiting. This traffic jam is in Mumbai, India.*

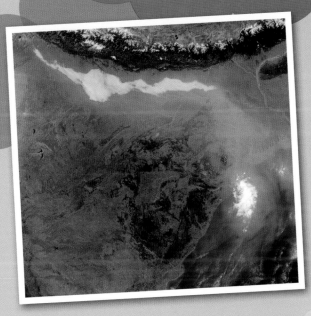

## The Asian brown cloud

The Asian brown cloud is a layer of air pollution that forms over southern Asia and eastern China every year from November to May. Scientists have noticed that the annual **monsoon** rains have started to arrive later since the development of the brown cloud, as the layer of pollution slows down the monsoon. This affects farming and reduces the amount of crops that can be grown.

*The brown cloud over northern India, as seen from space. When the monsoon rains come, the brown cloud is blown out over the ocean, where it breaks up.*

## Improvement

Air pollution in India is improving slowly. Although most cities still do not meet the country's targets for safe levels of air pollution, a few are making an effort. New rules aimed at reducing the fumes created by vehicles are helping to reduce toxic air on the streets. Natural gas, which creates less smoke than biomass, is becoming a popular fuel for cooking and heating.

## Politics

Air pollution in India is a political issue. Many people believe that the government is not doing enough to stop the worst polluting factories. More money needs to be invested in cities to improve public transportation and to clean up construction projects. Improving electricity supply in rural areas would help to cut down on pollution caused by burning biomass.

# Nuclear waste

**Radioactive** substances, such as uranium, are used as fuel in nuclear power plants. Nuclear power plants do not produce greenhouse gases, but the waste they produce is very hard to dispose of.

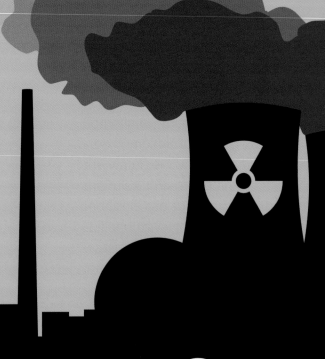

## Other uses

Uranium and other radioactive substances, such as radium, are also used in nuclear weapons and medical treatments. These also produce radioactive waste.

## Dangers

Nuclear waste is still radioactive after it has been used. Radioactive substances can make living things very sick if they get too close, so nuclear waste must be disposed of properly.

## Time

Nuclear waste remains radioactive for a long time after use. It must be kept in a shielded area until it stops being so dangerous. If it is in contact with water, air, or soil, it can **contaminate** the area around it.

Plutonium-239, used in nuclear weapons, remains radioactive for **24,110 years!**

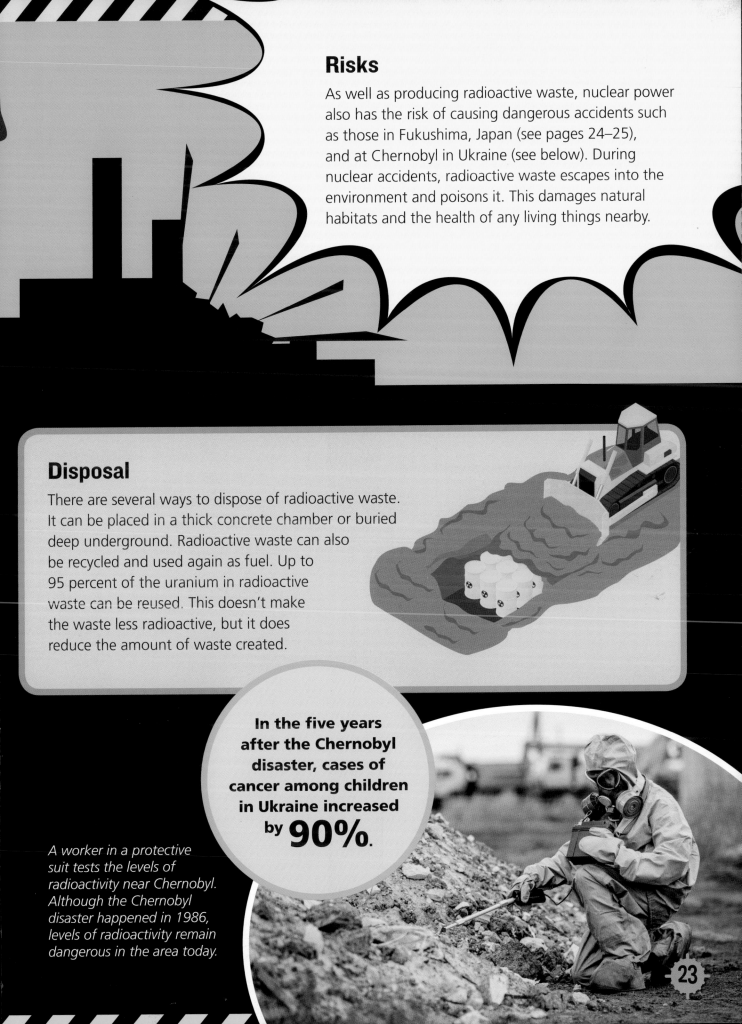

## Risks

As well as producing radioactive waste, nuclear power also has the risk of causing dangerous accidents such as those in Fukushima, Japan (see pages 24–25), and at Chernobyl in Ukraine (see below). During nuclear accidents, radioactive waste escapes into the environment and poisons it. This damages natural habitats and the health of any living things nearby.

## Disposal

There are several ways to dispose of radioactive waste. It can be placed in a thick concrete chamber or buried deep underground. Radioactive waste can also be recycled and used again as fuel. Up to 95 percent of the uranium in radioactive waste can be reused. This doesn't make the waste less radioactive, but it does reduce the amount of waste created.

In the five years after the Chernobyl disaster, cases of cancer among children in Ukraine increased **by 90%**.

*A worker in a protective suit tests the levels of radioactivity near Chernobyl. Although the Chernobyl disaster happened in 1986, levels of radioactivity remain dangerous in the area today.*

23

# Fukushima

In March 2011, a nuclear accident took place in Fukushima, Japan. After a devastating **tsunami**, the Fukushima Daiichi nuclear power plant went into **meltdown**, spreading radiation across the nearby land and ocean.

## FACT FILE

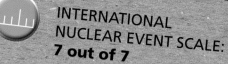

INTERNATIONAL NUCLEAR EVENT SCALE:
**7 out of 7**

RADIATION SPREAD:
**At least 28 miles (45 km)**

## Tsunami

On March 11, 2011, a very strong earthquake took place off the northeastern coast of Japan. The earthquake triggered a huge tsunami. Waves up to 30 feet (9 m) hit the coast of Japan 50 minutes after the earthquake. Over 22,000 people were killed. Over 1 million buildings were destroyed or damaged, including the Fukushima Daiichi nuclear power plant.

Tokyo

## Meltdown

In the days after the tsunami, all four **reactors** at the Fukushima Daiichi plant experienced meltdown. Heat built up inside the reactors and melted the fuel rods. The melted fuel rods burned through the protective layer surrounding the core and exposed it. Gas also built up and caught fire, causing an explosion that made a hole in the reactor. This allowed radiation to escape from the plant.

## Making it safe

The first step was to **stabilize** the reactors by cooling them down with water. Then workers fixed cracks to stop contaminated water from pouring into the sea or soil.

*Huge concrete covers were built over the reactors to block more radiation from escaping.*

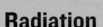

## Radiation

Despite the quick response, radiation from the Fukushima Daiichi plant spread across the surrounding land and sea. It seeped into the soil and contaminated plants. Crops that were being grown nearby at the time of the accident were destroyed. Radiation also flowed into the ocean. So far, it doesn't seem to have affected many ocean animals, but its effects are still being monitored.

## Evacuation

Immediately after the accident, people were evacuated from the area. Later, more areas were evacuated as the radiation spread through the air. Today, many areas have been declared safe to return to, but some people are too scared of the risks to go home.

## Long-term effects

So far, it is believed only one person has died from cancer caused by the Fukushima disaster. It is likely that the levels of radiation weren't high enough to cause serious damage, but people are still being monitored. The Fukushima site is still radioactive, and is not expected to be safe to reenter for another 30 years.

# Light and sound

**Too much light and sound damage the environment. They can affect human health, as well as animal behavior and navigation.**

## Threats

Light pollution can be disruptive for people. It can be hard to sleep properly if too much light enters the bedroom. It can also confuse **nocturnal** animals, such as owls, that sleep during the day and are active at night. If there is a lot of light during the night, nocturnal animals think that it is daytime and may continue to sleep.

## Light pollution

Light pollution is a major increase in the amount of light in an area, caused by artificial light. Artificial light comes from buildings and streetlights. Most light pollution happens in towns and cities.

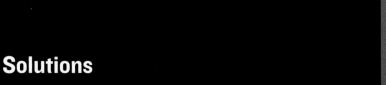

## Solutions

To reduce light pollution, people can turn off unnecessary lights when they leave a room or a building. Streetlights can be put on a timer so that they aren't on all night, or a sensor can be added so that the lights only turn on when people come close. Making these changes would reduce light pollution and electricity consumption, both of which are good for the environment.

**Do you know what happens to the lights at your school after everyone leaves? Find out and see if light sensors can be added.**

## Sound pollution

Sound pollution is loud or repetitive noise caused by machinery, vehicles, construction, or human activity, such as music. It can happen on land or on water. For example, ships and oil rigs cause sound pollution that affects ocean animals.

## Dangers of sound

Sound pollution affects humans in many ways. It can cause stress and sleeping problems, as well as more serious conditions, such as hearing loss. It can even lead to heart disease in extreme cases.

## Animals

Sound pollution can also affect animal behavior. It can stop them from reproducing and confuse them during hunting. Animals that use sound to navigate, such as bats, dolphins, and whales, struggle to find their way, as the sound pollution makes it hard for them to understand their surroundings. It can also change animal habitats, as animals move to new places to avoid noisy areas.

## Reducing noise

To help cut down on sound pollution, we can reduce the number of vehicles on the road. Governments can pass laws to control the working hours and amount of noise produced by factories and construction. Sound barriers can be built along highways and near airports to block sound pollution. To protect human health, houses should not be built near industrial areas or airports.

# Reducing pollution

Large companies and industries are mainly responsible for the pollution that threatens the planet. However, we can all help to reduce our impact on Earth.

## Reduce, reuse, recycle

Reducing the amount of objects we consume and reusing objects that we already have are the best ways of reducing waste. This cuts down on pollution created during the manufacturing process, as well as the waste that goes to landfill sites when we throw these objects away. Recycling is also important, but as the recycling process requires electricity, it's better to reduce and reuse first.

## One small step

**When you are finished with clothes, books, or toys, donate them to a charity instead of throwing them away.**

Carry a reusable water bottle

### Using less
There are many ways in which we can reduce and reuse at home and at school.

Buy loose fruits and vegetables

Store your sandwich loose in a lunchbox instead of wrapping it

Write or draw on scrap paper

## On the move

Cars create a huge amount of air pollution. Instead of using the car for short trips, why not walk or ride a bike? Public transportation, such as buses, does create some air pollution. However, it's still a better option than individual cars, as the pollution created per person is much less than if everyone on the bus drove their own car.

## Politics

It is the government's responsibility to control polluting industries and companies. Find out what your local representative is doing to prevent pollution. Ask them to address pollution in your area, if they aren't already.

## Speaking up

It can seem hard for us to make companies more environmentally friendly, but there are ways in which everyone can help. Join environmental charities, such as Greenpeace. Sign petitions and share information from this book with your friends and family. There is power in numbers. The more people that know and care about pollution, the more impact they will have.

*These volunteers are collecting garbage from a beach. Look for cleanup projects in your area and volunteer your time.*

CLEAN UP OUR PLANET!

NO MORE POLLUTION!

SAVE OUR PLANET!

STOP POLLUTION!

# Glossary

**algae** Living things that make much of Earth's oxygen

**atmosphere** The layer of gases around Earth

**biomass** Plants, wood, or dung used as fuel

**cargo** The goods carried by a ship

**carnivore** Animals and plants that eat meat

**climate change** A change in global climate patterns

**compost** Decayed organic matter used as fertilizer

**consume** To use up

**contaminate** To make something poisonous or less pure

**current** A flow of water directed by gravity

**decompose** To break down

**ecosystem** All the living things in an area

**environment** Natural surroundings

**fertilizer** A substance placed in the ground to make plants grow well

**fossil fuel** A fuel that comes from the ground, such as coal, oil, or gas

**greenhouse gas** A gas that traps heat in the atmosphere, such as carbon dioxide

**habitat** The natural home of a living thing

**harvest** To gather a crop

**herbivore** An animal that feeds on plants

**industry** The manufacture of goods for profit

**invest** To give money in order to help a business grow

**meltdown** An accident in a nuclear reactor in which fuel overheats and melts the core, releasing radiation into the environment

**monsoon** A season of heavy rain

**navigation** The ability to get from one place to another

**nocturnal** Describes an animal that becomes active at night

**photosynthesis** The process by which plants create energy using sunlight, water, and carbon dioxide

**plankton** Tiny living things in oceans that are important parts of food chains

**preserve** To protect and keep healthy

**radioactive** Describes something that gives off harmful radiation

**reactor** An apparatus in which nuclear reactions are controlled in order to produce nuclear energy

**rural** Relating to the countryside

**stabilize** To make something balanced and secure

**tidal power** The production of energy from the force of ocean waves

**tide** The natural rise and fall of oceans

**toxic** Poisonous

**tributary** A river or stream that flows into a larger river or lake

**tsunami** A giant ocean wave caused by an underwater earthquake or volcanic eruption

# Learning More

## Books

Dickmann, Nancy. *Leaving Our Mark: Reducing Our Carbon Footprint.* Crabtree Publishing, 2016.

Minay, Rachel. *Global Pollution.* Franklin Watts, 2018.

Rissman, Rebecca. *Reducing, Reusing, and Recycling Waste.* Crabtree Publishing, 2019.

## Websites

**www3.epa.gov/recyclecity/**
Play a game to learn more about recycling.

**https://climatekids.nasa.gov/air-pollution/**
Find out all about air pollution here.

**www.ducksters.com/science/environment/water_pollution.php**
Visit this site to learn more about water pollution.

# Index